M
J

How to Photograph Your World

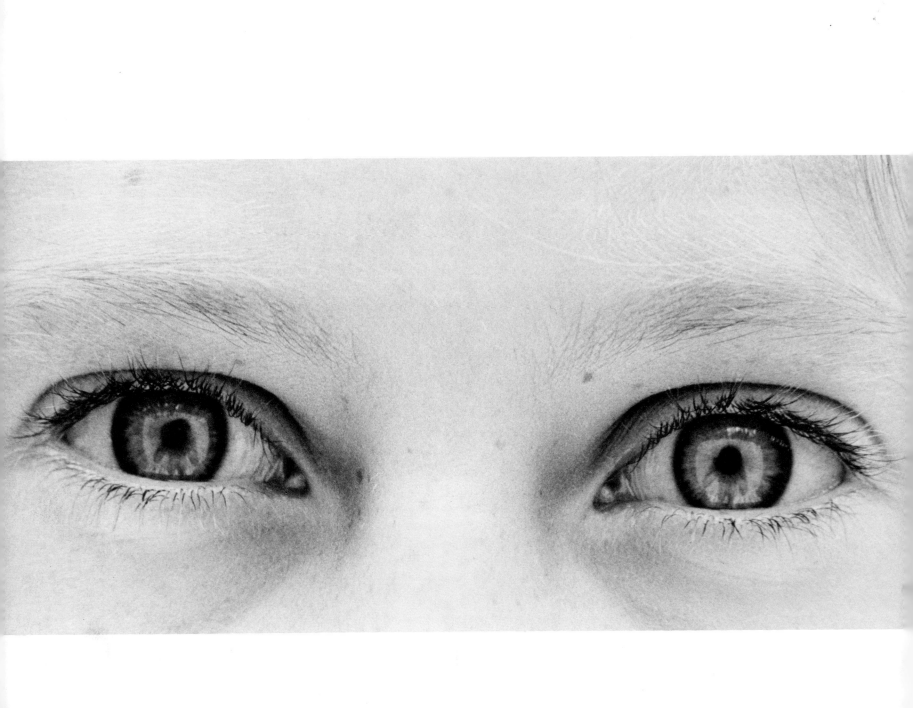

How to Photograph Your World
By VIKI HOLLAND

Photographs by the author

CHARLES SCRIBNER'S SONS, NEW YORK

To Morris, my love

CONTENTS

1. Seeing

The world you see is your own special world. There are many things in the world. You see only some of them. There are many ways to see the many things in the world. You see some of the things in the world with your own special way of seeing. Some people may think that everyone sees everything the same way. This is not true. The things you see and the way you see them are special. This is your way of seeing. It is your way of telling yourself what the world is all about.

Photography is a way of showing other people what you see. It is a way of letting people see the world through your eyes. If all your friends took a picture of the same thing—a puppy, a baby, or a tree—each picture would be different. Each pair of eyes sees a different world.

Your world is an important world. It is made up of all the things you have seen, all the things you have learned, and all the things that you remember. Some people do not see much of a world. They go around with their eyes on the ground. They probably know a lot about the cracks in the sidewalk and the shape of their toenails. If you are going to be a photographer and show your world to other people, then it is important to look a lot and to care a lot.

If you really look around you all the time—above you into the sky, below you onto the ground, close up to things so that your nose practically touches them, far away from things so that you can barely make them out—you will begin to get a good idea of what the world is all about.

Seeing means looking and then feeling and thinking about what you have seen. Seeing means getting to know things so that they feel like a part of you. If you get to know things very well, you can tell their story to everyone else with your photographs.

Change Your View

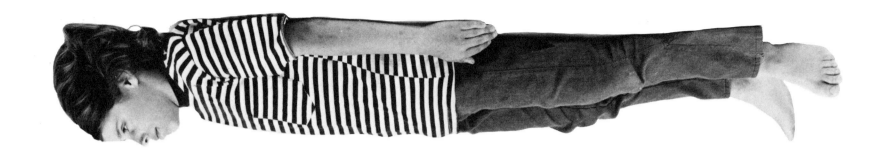

Look Close

Back Away

When you see with a camera, you must do some special things. The camera works very much like your eyes, but it is a machine and does not have the abilities of a living person. With your eyes, you can see the world clearly from six inches in front of your nose to the farthest horizon. A clear world is in focus. Compared to your eyes, the camera sees less of the world in focus.

A simple camera cannot focus on objects closer than four feet. A simple camera can only see the world in focus if it does not get too close to it. A complicated camera has a focusing dial with which you can put more or less of the world in or out of focus as you choose. With a complicated camera you can focus on things that are closer than four feet. The camera, however, cannot focus itself. You must decide what is in focus and what is out of focus for your camera.

The camera sees clearly only when it is very still. If you move the camera while you are taking a picture, the picture it sees and takes is blurred. One way to keep the camera very still is to keep yourself very still. To stand as still as you can, lock your knees and hold your breath.

If you want to see something special with a camera, you may have to wait for it to happen. Suppose that you want to catch a certain expression on a friend's face, or the yawn that your cat yawns when it first wakes up from its nap. You have to be patient and wait with your camera to capture those special things that you want to photograph. Take a friend along for company while you wait.

Your eyes see the world in color. Your camera can see the world in color or in black and white—depending on which type of film you put in your camera.

Color film comes in two types. One type makes color negatives from which you get colored photographic prints. The other type makes color transparencies; in order to look at them, you have to hold them up to the light or project them on a screen or wall with a slide projector.

Black and white photographs can tell a simple and powerful story. They are easier and less expensive for a beginner to make than color photographs. It might be wise to save your color film for events and objects in which the color is so striking that they say to you: "Photograph me in color."

You see with your eyes and with your mind. Your camera can record some of the things that you see. It sees the special things that you pick out of your world when you look through your camera at the world around you.

Move the Object

12

In Focus

Out of Focus

Stand Still

Be Patient

2. How Things Work

Light It may sound very strange, but you really do not see *things*. You see *light*. You see the light that such things as marbles, popsicles, or caterpillars reflect. Your eyes see patterns of light. Your mind takes that light and makes it into marbles, popsicles, or caterpillars. Light is what makes photography work. You use a camera to take the light that is reflected from the things in your world and to make pictures of those things to carry in your wallet or give to your friends.

The camera takes the light reflected from an object and puts it on a light-sensitive material called film. The film records the light. The film absorbs the light and holds on to it in an invisible picture. When the film is removed from the camera and processed through chemicals, the invisible picture becomes visible. The now visible picture is a negative.

Negatives are black and gray and transparent. They are the reverse of what your camera recorded. Everything that was dark in your world is now transparent on your negative. Everything that was light in your world is black on the negative, and everything in between is gray. A negative is the reverse of the world you photographed, with all the color taken out.

The negative is used to make a photographic print. The print looks just like the world you photographed. Prints are made by shining light through the negative onto a piece of light-sensitive paper. The paper holds an invisible image from the light shining through the negative, just as the film held an invisible image of the light shining through your camera lens. The light-sensitive paper is processed through the same type of chemicals as the film, and the picture you took becomes visible.

The negative is a picture of light recorded on film. The photographic print is a picture of light recorded on photographic printing paper. Light is what we see with our eyes, and light is what we use to make photographs. Pictures are products of our minds. We use the light our eyes see to construct pictures of our world—pictures of things like marbles, popsicles, and caterpillars.

The Camera The camera is a light-tight box. It has a hole in front covered with a special glass called a lens. The lens allows you to gather the light reflected from marbles, popsicles, or caterpillars and concentrate that light inside the box on your film.

Behind the lens is the diaphragm. The diaphragm controls how much of your lens is open to light. The diaphragm has a hole in its center that can be made smaller or larger depending on how much light you want to let into your camera. Inside the box, up against the back, there is a place for film. When you let the light in the lens it makes a picture on your film of whatever is in front of the lens of your camera.

Between the lens and the film, just behind the diaphragm, is the shutter. The shutter opens and closes each time you take a picture. The shutter controls how long you are letting light come through your lens, into your camera, and onto your film.

Your camera has a button that you press each time you take a picture. The button is called a shutter release. Each time you press the shutter release, the shutter opens and allows light to come in and record an image on your film. After the right amount of light has come in, the shutter closes. The length of time the shutter lets light into your camera is called the shutter speed.

Each time you press the shutter release, you record an image on your film of whatever is in front of your camera lens. These images are called exposures. They are the invisible pictures that your film holds on to until it is processed into negatives.

On the outside of your camera is a small window called the viewfinder. When you look through the viewfinder you can see the pictures you are recording as you press the shutter release.

On the top of your camera is a place for a flash unit. You attach a flash unit when you need extra light to take a picture. Flash units have small bright lights that go on when you press your shutter release. The lights make sure enough light is reflected to record your subject on film.

After you take each picture you roll your film to a fresh place with your film advance lever. Rolling your film to a new spot prevents you from recording two images on the same piece of film. A little window on the side of your camera shows you how many exposures you have left on your film and what kind of film you have in your camera.

Your camera has many parts. It has a lens which focuses light. It has a diaphragm which determines how much light gets through your lens. It has a shutter which determines how long the light enters your lens. It has a shutter release which opens and closes the shutter. It has a viewfinder which lets you see the picture you are taking. It has a flash unit which can add extra light when you need it, and it has a film advance lever which rolls the film you have used out of the way.

Cameras come in many models. Most of them are too complicated and expensive for beginners. The best beginner's camera is one that allows you to take pictures instead of getting bogged down in figuring out how your camera works.

One good camera for a beginner is a simple instant-loading camera. The instant-loading camera uses film that comes in a cartridge which you drop in the back of the camera. You do not have to worry about loading a roll of film into your camera. It has only one shutter speed (1/90th of a second) so you do not have to make decisions about what shutter speed to use. It has only one lens opening (*f11*) so you do not have to change your lens opening. It includes the whole world in focus (as long as you do not get closer than four or five feet to your subject). It is a fixed-focus camera.

It is a good idea to get a camera with a built-in light meter. This meter will read the light that is reflected from the objects you are photographing and allow your camera to operate only when the light is right. If you get a simple instant-loading camera with a built-in light meter, all you have to do is pick out your picture through your viewfinder, hold your camera very still, and gently press the shutter release. You can concentrate on what you see and on what picture to take.

If your camera does not have a built-in light meter, use the instructions that come with your film to decide whether there is enough light for your picture.

If someone in your family has a complicated camera that you are allowed to use, you can make it easier for yourself by converting it to a simple camera. Set the shutter speed on 1/100th, set the diaphragm on *f11,* and use the camera just like an instant-loading model until you have learned to find the pictures that you want to take.

While you are still learning to take photographs, it is probably best for you to have your film developed and your prints made by a professional photographic laboratory. Inquire at the camera store in your neighborhood about professional photo processing if you have special needs, or use the processing available at your local drug store until you become good enough to need a better service.

After you have been photographing a bit, perhaps you can sign up for a class in darkroom techniques at your school or park playground. If no class is available, you might persuade a local photographer to teach a group of young people like yourself how to develop your own pictures.

Types of Light

Bright Sun When the sun is very bright, the light has high contrast. There are places that are very light and there are shadows that are very dark. Strong light and dark create high contrast. When you take pictures in bright sun, make the dark and light work for you. Find a way to take your picture so that the things you want to see are in the sun and the things that can be hidden are in the shadow.

Indoors Inside houses and other buildings the light also has high contrast. This is because it is darker inside than it is outside. The light that comes from a window, door, or lamp makes a bright spot in a dim world. Take pictures indoors using the light that comes in the door or window to light up the most important part of your picture. If this is not enough light, use a flash unit.

Cloudy Bright When there are clouds over the sun, the light has low contrast. There are no deep shadows and no very bright spots of light. Cloudy bright is the easiest kind of light in which to take photographs. There are no shadows in your way, and people look nice because they do not have to squint against the sun.

Overcast On days when the sun is hidden away, the light has very low contrast and the light condition is called overcast. Pictures taken in overcast light can be very dull and gray. Try to find subjects with enough contrast in themselves when you are taking pictures on an overcast day.

Directions of Light

Side Light Side light models your subject. It gives you strong contrast between one side of the subject and the other. You get side light in bright sun and indoors when the light comes from one direction. Side light is good when you are photographing things with texture, like rough boards or cat's fur.

Back Light Back light occurs when the light source—such as the sun—is behind the subject. You use back light on very sunny days to avoid having your subject squinting into the sun. Back light sometimes makes your subject look gray and flat, but that is often better than having subjects with squinched-up faces. When you photograph in back light make sure the light source is not coming into your camera lens. Make sure that your subject blocks the light source, or the bright light can ruin your picture.

Speckled Light Speckled light has spots of dark and light. It happens under trees on bright sunny days. If you are careful, you can photograph people so that the sun makes a pattern for them to be in but does not make an important part of the subject too bright.

Diffuse Light Diffuse light comes from all around the subject. On cloudy bright or overcast days the light is diffuse. On the shady side of buildings on sunny days the light is diffuse. Take all the pictures that you want in any direction in diffuse light. The light is even and will not upset your photographs.

Front Light Front light comes from the sun or other light source shining directly on your subject. Direct front light can be used with objects that you want to appear very bright. Do not take pictures of people in direct front light. The bright light makes them squint and also makes their eyes look like dark holes. On sunny days, take your subjects into the shade or turn them around so that their backs are to the sun.

3. Taking Pictures

The most important thing to remember when you take a picture is to keep your fingers off the lens and your hands away from in front of the lens. Many fine pictures are ruined by large blurry globs which block out their most important parts. These globs are the photographer's hands. Fingers leave prints on the lens which will create blurred spots on all the pictures you take in the future. Keep your hands on the sides of the camera.

Another important thing to remember is to keep your camera horizontal. This means to keep it even so that one side of it doesn't tip toward the ground while the other side is tipping toward the sky. If you tip your camera, your pictures will look tilted. You might want to tip your camera sometimes to get a special effect, but make sure you do not tip it when you want it level.

Press your shutter release very gently so that you do not jerk the camera when you are taking a picture. Slowly press your finger on the button, and slowly release the button. Do not punch at it. This will jerk your camera and the movement will make your picture blur. Remember also to hold your breath.

You can help keep your camera still by bracing it on a convenient table, ledge, car fender, or door frame. Some people use a camera stand called a tripod to make sure their camera does not move. The camera screws onto the top of the tripod and allows you to take pictures without holding the camera yourself.

With an instant-loading or other fixed-focus camera, always remember to stand four or five feet away from your subject. Everything that is closer than four or five feet will come out blurred because your camera does not focus at close distances. Make sure that there is nothing in your picture that is closer than four feet.

Now that you are standing still, holding your breath, keeping your camera level and your hands away from in front of the camera, you are ready to gently press your shutter release and take your picture.

Have a Purpose

When you have a purpose, you decide what you are going to photograph. You choose something special and set out to take pictures of what you have chosen. You might decide to photograph something or someone you have known for a long time. You might decide to photograph your dog or cat. Sometimes interesting things happen and you have to decide instantly that you are going to photograph the event right then and there. This is what happened to my daughter Molly and myself.

One day a baby possum fell into the kitchen window and landed behind the vegetable steamer on the stove. He had lost his mother and was looking for food. He made a great racket when he landed, and we ran into the kitchen and discovered him crouched in the corner. We named him Zork and decided to take his picture.

Plan Ahead

If you plan ahead you will catch photographs that are easily missed. One way to plan ahead is to keep your camera loaded with film. Another way is to keep your camera in the same place all the time so you do not have to look for it. When you have a specific purpose you can sometimes plan ahead and set up a situation for the picture you want to occur. In this way you can anticipate what your subject is going to do and get there ahead of time. For example, if you know that your new puppy gets his droopy ears in his food bowl when he eats, you can stand by with camera loaded and ready to shoot as soon as you feed him. You can then catch a photograph of him coming up with his ears dripping dog food.

Molly and I planned ahead when we decided to take pictures of Zork. We knew that we would have to be very careful or he would run away. We wanted to entice him into a position that would be easy to photograph. First we blocked off the stove with large cereal boxes so that Zork was forced to climb up on a shelf with an open box of chamomile tea on it. Since there was no other place that he could go, we knew he would climb into the box. We hoped that he would curl up and go to sleep in the box. Our planning worked out. He climbed into the box and went to sleep. We moved him outside very gently so that we could get better pictures of him.

Wait for the Action

Sometimes it takes a while for the right picture to happen. It is important to be patient and wait. If you stand around long enough something usually does happen. Sometimes you have to talk to subjects to help loosen them up. It takes time for people to loosen up. It takes time for things to happen, and so it takes time to take good pictures.

After Molly and I carried the chamomile tea box outside, we waited for Zork to wake up. We knew we would get a funny picture of him with his head popping out of the tea box. We waited quite a while.

Encourage Your Subject

Both people and animals are timid about having their pictures taken. The best thing to do is to soothe them and make them feel good about themselves. If you want to take pictures of people, compliment them. Tell them how much you care about them and how nice a picture of them would be. If you want to make friends with an animal, feed it, pet it, and be gentle with it all the time. Living things like to be cared about. If you care about your pictures, care about your subjects.

Molly and I noticed that Zork was very frightened. Molly asked her dad to pick him up and make him feel cozy. Some animals bite when they are frightened. Do not pick up an animal unless you know it well.

28

Sneak Around

Sometimes live subjects get self-conscious if you aim a camera directly at them. They get stiff and their pictures come out looking funny. Once in a while you might sneak around in back or to the side and take their picture when they are not aware of what you are doing. You can get more natural pictures this way. Be careful not to invade someone's privacy when you do this. Do not photograph people who would object.

Molly decided to sneak around and take Zork's picture. She kept herself in back of him and out of his sight. It worked. He didn't run away.

WATCH THE BACKGROUND!

Although you select the world you see, the camera sees everything in the world. If you get excited about photographing your subject, you may see only that subject. You may not notice that all around the subject are distracting objects. You may not realize that your picture will be ruined by a background that is too busy. The camera records all the things in front of the lens when you press the shutter release. It does not decide whether things look good or not. All the messy, busy things that you did not notice will be there in the picture.

Look carefully through your viewfinder before you take a picture. Make sure there is nothing in front of your lens that will detract from what you want to say.

Molly took a picture of Zork on a clean shelf outside the kitchen window. Then she put all sorts of junky, messy things around Zork and took his picture again. You can hardly find Zork in the mess. It is important to keep your background simple if you want what you have to say to be seen.

Molly changed the angle at which she took her picture. In the picture with the simple background she shot down on Zork because he was all curled up in the box. In the messy picture she shot straight on so that it would be even harder to find him in the mess.

You can control how your picture looks and what it says both by making sure that your background is very simple and by deciding on the best shooting angle (use a stepladder or stand in a hole—if one is handy!).

4. Composing Pictures

Composing pictures is looking at the things in the world in many different ways, from many different angles, until you find the picture that says what you want to say. You can compose a picture in the viewfinder of your camera and then make an exposure of that composition. You can also compose a picture after you get your prints back from the photo lab.

To compose a picture from a print, you crop the print to include only the parts that you want in your picture. Cropping means to cut the picture down. You keep what you want and cut out the excess. After you have decided what part of the print you want to keep, mark it on the print you got from the processor. Return the marked print and the negative to the photo lab. They will take your negative and make a print from it that includes only the part you marked on the print. The photo lab makes you a new print from the cropped instructions.

When you compose a picture, you can arrange the parts of the picture to say special things. There are patterns in the world that make what you want to say come out stronger and clearer. Pictures of square things like boxes and doorways say "neat." Pictures of round things like balls and oranges say "complete." Pictures

of big things like elephants say "strong." Pictures of small things like kittens say "helpless." Pictures of far-away things give you room to dream. Pictures of close-up things demand your attention—they crowd you. Pictures of dark things are brooding. Pictures of light things are airy. Pictures of vertical things like skyscrapers are energetic and striving. Pictures of horizontal things like the horizon over the ocean have a stillness and peace—they are rooted in the earth.

While you are taking pictures, find things that help you say what you want to say. How do you say "busy"? How do you say "happy"? Find a way.

The most important thing about composing a picture is to keep it simple. The simpler your picture, the clearer what you are saying will be. To keep your picture simple, decide what is important in the picture and leave everything else out. If there are things in your way, try shooting down on your subject from above, or up on your subject from below. Either of these viewpoints may help to simplify your background and make your subject come out stronger and clearer.

Make sure all the parts of your pictures go

together. Make sure they do not fight with each other. When you are looking through your viewfinder, check to see if any part of your picture disagrees with any other part. Sometimes things fight with each other because there are too many of them. Sometimes they fight because they are all running off in different directions. Make sure that all the parts of your picture help tell the world the main things that you want to say.

There are many different ways in which each picture can be composed. You can take a picture from many different angles, or viewpoints, and its composition will change. Composing pictures is something you do. You do it deliberately and carefully. Composing pictures is a way of organizing and telling about your world.

Uncomposed

Composed

Patterns

People in Patterns

Square

Round

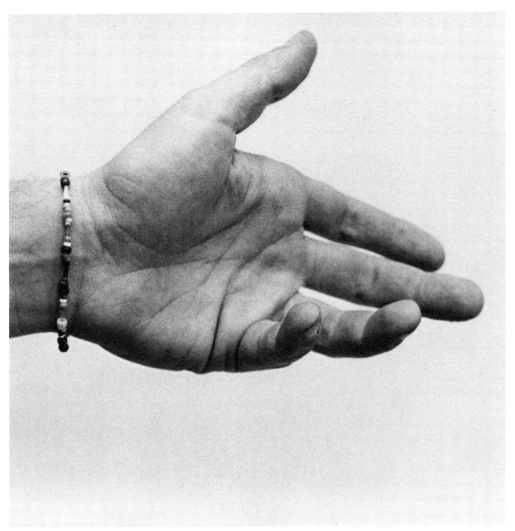

Big

Small

Far

Near

Dark

Light

Vertical

Horizontal

5. Your World—Find It

All around you is a very exciting world. It is the world you live in and know better than anyone else alive. It is the world you see with your eyes, touch with your fingers, hear with your ears, taste with your tongue, and remember from yesterday and way back last summer.

Your world is full of people. Those people may be your parents, your sisters and brothers, your aunts and uncles, your friends and neighbors. All sorts of people who come in every size and shape. Find the people you care about. Try to understand what it is about them that best expresses who they are. Wait until they look just like that and then snap—take their picture. They are your people. You can take great pictures of them.

There are houses on your street, dogs on your street, and kids with tricycles. Find out what is special about them and record it with your camera. There is junk on your street, litter on your street, sad people on your street. See if you can tell their story with your camera. There is a whole world of leaves and trees, of flowers and birds, trucks and trains, buildings and fire hydrants.

In the city, in the country, in the small town, and in the suburbs there is a beautiful, ugly, simple, complicated, round, square, up, down, loud, soft world waiting for you to photograph.

Go out into your world and look. Find out what is odd about it. Odd things are things that make you stop and think twice. Odd things make good pictures.

Find out what is usual in your world. Usual things are things that happen every day. Everyday things make us feel safe and secure. Everyday things are good to photograph. They make us feel good about our world.

Find out what is active in your world. Photograph the little league, the ocean, people playing stick ball. Active things tell us what we do. If you want to show speed, photograph a moving car and see how the blur on your film says "speed."

Find out what is quiet in your world. Take pictures of rocking chairs waiting for people to come and sit in them, doorbells waiting to be rung, leaves lying silently on the ground. Tell the story of being quiet.

Find your world. Photograph it.

You

Family

People
at Work

Animals

6. Your World—Make It

Sometimes you have ideas inside your head that you would like to photograph. Make them happen. You can take different parts of the world and put them together to show the idea that you have inside your head. Take different things in your world and put them together in pleasing patterns. Take fruit in a bowl, parts of machinery, or collections of shells, and arrange them in a way that says what you want to say about these objects.

Sometimes you have ideas about people. You would like them to be princes or pirates or astronauts. Dress them up and take their pictures. One way to take good pictures of people is to frame them in some way so that they stand out. You can frame someone in a window or doorway.

Make a mood to take a picture in. Make a mood that is dark and brooding. Make the background dark and the people sad and lonely. Make a picture that is light and airy. Make it white and wispy. You can do this by having a light background and dressing your subject in fabrics that are sheer and light.

Get your friends to pose for you. Take pictures of them hamming it up. Tell their story by surrounding them with props that tell who they are. A prop can be a baseball bat and mitt for a friend who plays the game. A prop can be a chocolate soda for a friend who guzzles them down all the time. A prop can be a horse that a little girl loves more than anything else in the world besides her family and friends. Find out what your friends are interested in and take their pictures using props to tell their story. Make your world happen with your camera.

Compose pictures that tell how you feel about things. If you care about our environment take pictures of cans littering the highway or of your friends choking on a smoggy day.

If you care about people getting together, take pictures of all different kinds of people working and playing together. If you want to have some fun, make up some pictures that do not seem possible—trick pictures.

There are lots of pictures in the world that you can make because you imagined them, you put them together, and you cared about them.

Framing

Hamming

Props

Tricks

Funny Faces

7. Tell a Story

You can tell a story with a series of pictures that go together. Find some event that is interesting and arrange to be there with your camera as the event happens.

A story has a beginning, a middle, and an end. When you are taking your pictures, make sure that you get pictures that show how the story begins, what happens as it progresses, and how it ends. A story should have a particular theme that you make the most important thing in your story. It can be a hero. A hero is a person who does something very special. It can be a good deed. It can be a strange thing that doesn't happen very often, like a flower that blooms every one hundred years.

You can take pictures of little details that make your story seem more real. If your story takes place in a house, you might want a picture of the doorway to let you into the house. You might want a picture of the kind of plants that grow around the house. You can use details to help tell your story.

Most important of all, tell a story that you care about.

A few years ago, some young people I know decided to help some very old people on their street to paint their house. The young people arranged to get the paint, equipment, and most of the labor, and I promised to take pictures. Here is the story of "The House on 107th Street."

Our neighbors' house needed painting

We offered
to help paint it

The whole neighborhood turned out

We painted ourselves

We painted the house

8. Show Your World to Others

After you have taken a number of pictures that you like, you can display them for others to see. You can put them in a scrapbook or in your wallet. You can put them in small picture frames that sit on people's desks and night tables. There are plastic cubes in the photo stores that display four or five pictures at once, and there are all sorts of frames that you can buy and build to hang your pictures on the wall.

One way that I display my pictures is to put them in old frames that I collect in junk stores and antique shops. I carefully match my picture to a frame and make a print that will fit the frame. Then I hang the pictures in groups on the wall.

This is one way of showing other people what you see.

Displaying your pictures is a way of letting others see the world through your eyes.